C000174592

THE RAILWAYS OF THE REPUBLIC OF IRELAND 1925-75

also in this series

EUROPEAN STEAM IN ACTION
AUSTRIAN STEAM FROM LINESIDE
STEAM ON BRITAIN'S MINIATURE RAILWAYS
MINERAL RAILWAYS OF THE WEST COUNTRY
CORNWALL'S RAILWAYS — A PICTORIAL SURVEY
SCOTTISH STEAM IN THE 1920s
MEMORIES OF STEAM AROUND BRITAIN
PORTUGESE STEAM FROM LINESIDE
BR STANDARD STEAM IN ACTION
SPECIALS IN ACTION
BRITISH NARROW GAUGE STEAM — A PICTORIAL SURVEY
EUROPEAN NARROW GAUGE STEAM — A PICTORIAL SURVEY
INDUSTRIAL NARROW GAUGE RAILWAYS IN BRITAIN
SOUTH AMERICAN STEAM — A PICTORIAL SURVEY
STEAM IN THE ANDES
NEW ZEALAND STEAM SPECTACULAR
ARTICULATED LOCOMOTIVES OF THE WORLD
VULCAN FOUNDRY LOCOMOTIVES 1834-1956
STEAM SUPER-POWER AROUND THE WORLD

THE **RAILWAYS** OF THE REPUBLIC OF **IRELAND**

A PICTORIAL SURVEY OF THE G.S.R. AND C.I.E. 1925-75

Michael H. C. Baker

D. BRADFORD BARTON LIMITED

 ISBN 085153 2357

Published by Roberts Wholesale Books Limited
Unit 12, Benson Street Enterprise Centre, Hanover Quay, Dublin 2

Printed and bound in Great Britain by BPC Hazell Books Ltd

introduction

The Great Southern Railways Company came into existence on 1 January 1925, being a not altogether willing but a financially necessary amalgamation of no less than 26 concerns. The only ones left out were those which operated across the border into Northern Ireland, much the most important of these being the Great Northern.

Twenty years later, in 1945, CIE (Corias Iompair Eireann) was created out of the Great Southern and the Dublin United Transport Company. In 1950 CIE was nationalised, bringing together all forms of public road, rail and water transport operating entirely within the Republic of Ireland. The GNR continued on its independent—but now faltering—way until September 1958 when what remained of it was divided between the Ulster Transport Authority and CIE; since that date, all public railways within the 26 Counties have belonged to CIE.

The Great Southern can hardly be said to have been born with a silver spoon in its corporate mouth. The Irish Free State in 1925 had barely recovered from the bitter years of the struggle for Independence and the following Civil War immediately thereafter and throughout its twenty years the Great Southern waged a losing battle with the motor vehicle. Consequently there was little money for new rolling stock and only 60 locomotives plus 128 coaching vehicles were built between 1925 and 1945. From the antiquarian's point of view this was splendid, for many ancient specimens survived beyond what would have been considered their allotted life span anywhere else. Thus CIE inherited a locomotive and carriage stock whose average was 48 and 44 years respectively; that of the wagons was an almost respectable 29.

CIE tentatively embarked on dieselisation in 1947 with five shunters, followed by two main line locomotives in 1951. Later that year the first railcars arrived and the end of steam was at hand. There had been some steam railcars in the 1920's as well as the famous Drumm battery electrics of the 1930's, but the AEC/Park Royal diesel cars, based closely on those introduced by the GNR in 1950, were the first real break-through.

In 1955 wholesale delivery of diesel-electric locomotives began, first from England—principally Crossley-engined Metropolitan Vickers—then some shunters from Germany, and finally the highly successful General Motors Bo-Bos from the USA. *Maeve*, the most famous and most powerful locomotive—steam or diesel—ever to run in Ireland, worked her last train in 1958 and was subsequently moved to the Transport Museum in Belfast. Steam working on CIE ended altogether in 1965, other than for occasional outings by preserved engines, chiefly those belonging to the Railway Preservation Society of Ireland.

Since then, diesel traction has been the rule on CIE, but with an increasing awareness of the necessity of an efficient railway system the long-mooted electrification of the Dublin suburban lines grows nearer. Some form of underground railway is likely to be linked with this. Equally exciting, although a longer term possibility, is the electrification of the Dublin-Cork main line.

After decades of neglect, the future of the railways in the 26 Counties is assured and CIE can look forward to an increasing share of both goods and passenger traffic throughout the country.

Kingsbridge in the early 1900's, successively the headquarters of the GSWR, the GSR and nov CIE. Designed by Sancton Wood and completed in 1844, Kingsbridge, which was renamed Heusto in 1966 after one of the leaders of the 1916 Uprising, is by general consent the finest piece of railwa architecture in Ireland. A contemporary account describes its position as 'peculiarly desirable' o account of its proximity to the warehouses and quays, but the Victorian centre of Dublin is nov run-down, business and social life having moved eastwards leaving Heuston almost in the suburbs At one time it was closed down on Sundays but the revised and expanded timetable of 1973 ha transformed Heuston. A new island platform has been added, making five in all and today it i busier than at any time in its history. [National Library of Ireland

Broadstone, the imposing granite terminus of the Midland Great Western Railway. Whilst architecturally fit to ran with Kingsbridge, on the opposite bank of the Liffey, traffic here was never heavy and by 1937 the GSR had foun it possible to divert all of it to the more centrally placed Amiens Street and Westland Row of the former Dublin an South Eastern Railway. The locomotive shed here remained until the end of steam in 1961 but the station and workshop were handed over to CIE's road services. Today, although little changed externally since its completion in 1847, Broad stone is the headquarters of CIE's Provincial Road Fleet. [National Library of Ireland

GREAT SOUTHERN & WESTERN RAILWAY

Dun Laoghaire station, formerly Kingstown, was the southern terminus of the Dublin & Kingstown, the first railway in Ireland. The engine is CIE C2 Class 4-4-2T No. 455. She was built by the DSER in 1911 as No. 20 and to celebrate Coronation year was named *King George*. She was the last locomotive to be built at the company's Grand Canal Street works, an establishment which 70 years earlier had produced the first locomotive in the world to be built by a railway company at its own works. By 1911, Grand Canal Street was so cramped and inadequate that a good deal of the assembly of *King George* had to be done in the running shed opposite and no-one was surprised when one of the first acts of the GSR was to close Grand Canal Street down. No. 455 was withdrawn in 1959. [CIE]

The Dublin & Kingstown expanded to become first the Dublin, Wicklow & Wexford and then, on completion of the Waterford line, the Dublin & South Eastern Railway. The main line from Dublin to Rosslare closely follows the coast and as a consequence abounds in gradients and curves. Here a train negotiates one of the sections sometimes actually covered by the sea at exceptionally high tides, along the quay at Wexford.
[H. C. Casserley]

Rosslare Harbour, the south-eastern extremity of the GSR and CIE systems. In this view in 1938 the funnel of a GWR steamer can be seen in the background whilst 4-4-2T No. 271 shunts a variety of wagons, including a former MGWR horse-box, complete with dog kennel. No. 271 was originally No. 18 *Geraldine* of the Waterford, Limerick and Western Raliway, a company absorbed by the GSWR in 1901. *Geraldine*'s designer was J. G. Robinson who was in charge of the Limerick works immediately before moving back to Gorton in England and the Great Central.
[H. C. Casserley]

Waterford. Another designer who became famous across the water was R. E. L. Maunsell. He began his career as a C.M.E. at Inchicore, moving to Ashford immediately before the First World War. Here one of his large J4 0-6-0s, No. 263, sets off with a goods for Wexford. The photograph dates from 1959, four years before No. 263's withdrawal.
[David Murray]

Waterford. Across the River Suir and remote from the rest of the Irish system, the last single in ordinary service in the British Isles sets out from Riverside station for Tramore in June 1932. No.483, a 2-2-2WT, was built by Fairburns in 1855 and might well have attained her century for she had been overhauled by the GSR and was an economical and efficient machine. Unfortunately, a serious accident in 1936 led to her withdrawal a year later. [H. C. Casserley]

Westward again, along the coast to Cobh, formerly Queenstown. In this photograph, taken in July 1934, one of the celebrated J15 0-6-0s sets off for Cork with a corridor train. Tied up alongside the station are the tenders used to ferry passengers to and from the Atlantic liners which, in the days before air travel, called regularly at Cobh. [H. C. Casserley]

To this day, the railway has a monopoly of suburban traffic between Cobh and Cork. In this scene in 1924, another J15 pulls out of Tivoli station with a train of six-wheelers. The J15 was the most numerous class in Ireland; 111 were built between 1866 and 1901, nearly all of which survived into CIE days. Some were active on the last day of steam and two have been preserved. [Rex Murphy]

A Cobh train alongside the River Lee at the time of the 1925 Amalgamation. The locomotive is a GSWR mixed traffic D4 4-4-0, No. 334, designed by Coey, Maunsell's predecessor at Inchicore. The up-to-date corridor stock and the luggage vans at the rear suggest the train is a through boat express from Dublin. Eight D4s were built in 1907/8 and a further five by the GSR in 1936. No. 334 was withdrawn in 1955. [Rex Murphy]

Glanmire Road station, Cork, in 1932. The engine is No. 17, an Aspinall 4-4-0 of 1888. Aspinall was yet another designer who went to England, leaving Inchicore in the early 1890's for the Lancashire & Yorkshire. Glanmire Road, renamed Kent in 1966, is a busy station with an all-over roof, two through platforms and four terminal ones, plus two through goods lines which pass outside the station.

[H. C. Casserley]

A photograph recalling the withdrawal of the British Forces from Ireland in 1922. A train ferry, complete with travelling crane, loads military equipment from the quayside at Cork. Note the locomotive in front of the large warehouse on the opposite quay. Trains still run through the streets and along the docksides of Cork, connecting Kent station with that of the former Cork, Bandon and South Coast Railway at Albert Quay.
[Walter McGrath collection]

A scene at the GSWR shed, Cork, situated between the south end of Glanmire Road station and the River Lee. This picture, taken in GSWR days, is of particular interest in being one of the few known to have been taken of a 'Long Tom', Ireland's first 4-6-0s. Some railwaymen and their friends from the Royal Irish Constabulary are posed in front of No. 363. There were six of these Coey goods engines, built between 1905 and 1907. Although powerful, they were heavy on coal and the money-conscious Great Southern soon withdrew them, the class being extinct by 1931.
[Walter McGrath collection]

Albert Quay in GSR days when this was the terminus for the West Cork lines; a train for Bantry leaves behind an Inchicore-built C4 Class 4-4-2T of 1901 and a CBSCR 4-6-0T. There were eight of these latter engines, powerful machines built by Beyer Peacock between 1906 and 1920. Although chiefly to be found in Cork, examples worked on the Dublin suburban services for a number of years. The last two survived the closure of the West Cork lines, apart from Albert Quay which is still in use as a freight depot, and were not withdrawn until 1965. [Walter McGrath]

Two pictures taken during the Civil War of 1922–3: above, officials inspect a damaged bridge in West Cork. Be a troop train on the Cork & Macroom Direct Railway. The soldiers are clearing away the debris of an ambush days earlier. During the Civil War, the railways were constantly under attack all over the country and suffered h damage. Rolling stock was destroyed, many lines were out of action for months and when the war was over the State Government paid out many thousands of pounds in compensation. [Walter McGrath collec

A number of minor railways, all now vanished, once operated in County Cork. This scene is of Ballydehob in the far south-west in 1918. In the foreground is the station of the narrow gauge Schull & Skibbereen Railway; across the valley is the village church. This latter and the impressive viaduct remain, although the railway closed in 1947. [Walter McGrath collection]

The 3ft gauge Cork & Muskerry Light Railw operated to the north-west of Cork city. Her train leaves Blarney Castle station headed b Brush-built 4-4-0T No *Dripsey* in July 1934, the last summer of the line's operation. No.8 lasted from 1904 to 193 [H. C. Casser

One of the two 3ft gauge lines to be found within Cork city was that of the former Cork, Blackrock & Passage Railway. This had been converted from standard to narrow gauge in 1899, but tram and later bus competition eventually took most of its traffic and the Great Southern closed it down in 1933. This 1932 view is of the only double track section of narrow gauge line in Ireland. The engine, 2-4-2T No. 7, was transferred on the line's closure to the Cavan & Leitrim section and worked there for a further 21 years.
[H. C. Casserley]

North of County Cork lies what is known as the Kingdom of Kerry. A county of great beauty, this contains Ireland's chief tourist attraction, the lakes of Killarney. Here jaunting cars—still a familiar sight—and carriages line up outside the GSWR station at Killarney in Edwardian times in anticipation of the arrival of a train from Dublin. [National Library of Ireland]

Arguably the most spectacular rail journey in Ireland was that on the narrow gauge line which ran from Tralee along the Dingle peninsula to Dingle town. Here a cattle train, headed by Hunslet-built 2-6-0Ts Nos. 1 and 2, pauses at Castlegregory Junction. After passenger services ended in 1939, the cattle fair at Dingle provided the line with traffic for another fourteen years. Nos. 1 and 2, built in 1889, were scrapped when the line closed but another of the Tralee & Dingle engines survives in the USA. [*The Cork Examiner*]

A line which contributed more than most to Ireland's reputation for eccentric modes of transport was the Listowel & Ballybunion monorail in County Kerry. The brainchild of a Frenchman, Charles Lartigue, it was closed three months before the GSR came into existence, chiefly, it is said, because that company refused to have anything to do with something so peculiar. In this view one of its double-boilered Kitson-built engines stands beside the shed at Ballybunion.
[Deegan Photography]

The most north-westerly outpost of the Great Southern was Sligo. A Sligo, Leitrim & Northern Counties Railway railbus prepares to set out from the GSR station there for Enniskillen, 43 miles away across the Northern Ireland border in County Fermanagh, in 1945. The avowedly anti-railway attitude of the Six Counties government in the 1950's brought about the end of the SLNCR, but Sligo continues to be served by CIE trains.
[Walter McGrath]

Achill, terminus of another remote MGWR branch, closed in 1937. The engine is one of the long-lived former GSWR D17 4-4-0s, No. 57, built in 1888 and withdrawn in 1957.
[H. C. Casserley]

Clifden was the terminus of the former MGWR line from Galway, running through the magnificient but sparsely populated scenery of Connemara. Its greatest moment came when it conveyed Alcock and Brown, who landed near Clifden after their epic flight across the Atlantic in 1919. This 49-mile-long branch was closed in 1935, a year after this photograph was taken. The engine, J18 0-6-0 No. 589, was built at Broadstone in 1892 and withdrawn in 1963.
[H. C. Casserley]

Of the 563 locomotives taken over by the GSR in 1925, 311 came from the GSWR. One third of all these were J15 0-6-0s which found their way to every corner of the GSR system and were employed on every type of duty from hauling express passenger trains to heating empty stock. No. 140, a much-rebuilt 1881 engine, seen here hurrying a ballast train along the main line near Mallow in CIE days, remained in service for 80 years. [David Murray]

A further 82 of the former GSWR engines were 4-4-0s of various types, the most powerful being No. 341 *Sir William Goulding*. An air of mystery surrounds the history of this locomotive. The only express engine built by Maunsell whilst he was at Inchicore, No. 341 was obviously meant to be something out of the ordinary and was named after the company chairman. She was apparently well able to haul the heaviest trains and was popular with her crews, but the GSR had little use for her and withdrew her in 1929 after a mere 16 years' service. No. 341 was, however, not immediately broken up but put to work as a stationary boiler at Inchicore.

The successor to *Sir William Goulding* was No. 400. E. A. Watson came from Swindon to succeed Maunsell in 1913 and No. 400 was intended to be his masterpiece, an improved Star. Although there were certain similarities to the GWR engines, performance was not one of them and No. 400 proved so unsatisfactory that she was scrapped the same year as *Sir William Goulding*. Meanwhile nine further engines of the class had been built. Two of these were also withdrawn by the GSR whilst the others were heavily rebuilt. No. 406, which ended her days as a two-cylinder engine with Caprotti valve gear, is seen passing Inchicore with the Radio Train in June 1954. She was withdrawn in 1957. [David Murray]

The rebuilding of the 400s was influenced by the success of the two-cylinder 500 Class mixed-traffic 4-6-0s of J. R. Bazin, Watson's successor. No. 500 came out in 1924 and Nos. 5001/2 under the GSR two years later. No doubt there would have been more had it not been for the advent of the cost-price Woolwich class. The 500s spent their lives on Dublin–Cork expresses and here No. 501 heads through Clondalkin on the outskirts of Dublin with the down Night Mail on a June evening in 1952, three years before her withdrawal.
[David Murray]

The GSR inherited a small, but motley collection of largely antiquated tank engines. Narrow gauge ex-Cavan & Leitrim 4-4-0T No. 3 of 1887 now preserved in the USA.
[Dr. E. M. Patterson]

Narrow gauge ex-West Clare 0-6-2T No. 5 of 1892, preserved at Ennis.
[Michael H. C. Baker]

There could hardly be a greater contrast between the diminutive specimens opposite and the massive eight-coupled locomotive here in the yard at Kingsbridge. No. 900 was built in 1915, a sister engine following nine years later. They were the only eight-coupled engines to run on the standard gauge in Ireland but, like so many of the larger GSWR designs, fell into disfavour with the Great Southern. Their long, rigid wheelbase damaged the tracks in the Kingsbridge yard where they worked; although as can be seen here No. 900 operated for a time as a 4-6-2T, this did little to alleviate the trouble and she was scrapped in 1928. No. 901 had a quite remarkably short life of seven years. [Real Photographs]

The second largest company absorbed by the Great Southern, the MGWR, worked most of its passenger services with 4-4-0s and 2-4-0s. The latter, the G2s, were of particular interest in that they were the most powerful engines of that wheel arrangement in the British Isles. Built between 1893 and 1898, all 20 of them—with the exception of one damaged beyond repair during the Civil War—survived into the 1950's. Above, No. 666 in original condition with Atock 'fly-away' cab, stands on the turntable at Broadstone in 1929. No. 666 saw service from 1897 to 1957. Below, No. 658 (1898–1954), with round-topped cab, on a Cavan train at Mullingar in 1932. [H. C. Casserley]

No. 653, seen in final condition shunting at Galway in 1959, was built in 1894 and was the last of the class to be withdrawn in 1963. [Michael H. C. Baker]

The Great Southern twice attempted to provide modern motive power for the Dublin suburban services. In 19
No. 850 appeared, a large 2-6-2T with 5ft 6in driving wheels and, so it is said, certain parts of the 27th, never assembl
Woolwich 2-6-0. In 1933 the five I 3 0-6-2Ts came out. Neither type was entirely successful and the motley collecti
of pre-Amalgamation tank and tender engines continued to predominate until dieselisation in the 1950's. No. 850 w
withdrawn in 1955, No. 674 in 1959. [Kevin Murra

The most modern MGWR engines were the 26 Woolwich 2-6-0s, the first of which was under construction at Broadstone Works at the time of the Amalgamation. Their purchase—unassembled—from the Woolwich Arsenal, brought more Maunsell-designed engines into the GSR fold than had come from his own GSWR. No. 397, one of the later engines with 6ft driving wheels—the equivalent of the Southern Railway N 1 Class—leaves Mallow in June 1953 with a Cork–Rosslare boat train. The second carriage is a former Pullman, one of four introduced in 1926 and bought by the GSR ten years later; the fourth is one of the 66ft long clerestories built for this service in 1906. No. 397 ran from 1930 to 1957. [David Murray]

850
674

From its inception, the Grea
Southern experimented with
forms of motive power other
than the conventional steam
engine in an attempt to incre
efficiency and reduce costs.
No. 281 was one of two small
Sentinel shunters which wor
from 1927 to 1948.
[H. C. Casse

Four Drewry petrol-engined four-wheel railcars entered service in 1927/8. Two were narrow gauge cars, for the West Clare Section: No. 386 was one of the standard gauge cars, here seen at Goolds Cross when working the Cashel branch in 1928.
[*The Cork Examiner*]

The GSR also operated ten much larger bogie steam rail-cars. Four were Sentinels with 55-seat bodies. No. 357 stands at Newmarket in February 1928, a few months after delivery from the Shrewsbury works. Like its sisters it was scrapped in 1941/2. [*The Cork Examiner*]

Less successful were the six Clayton cars of 1928. They were all out of service by the end of 1931, and, with the locomotive sections removed, were converted to three two-car sets of articulated trailer carriages for the Waterford-Tramore line. No. 360 stands outside Mullingar shed in September 1929, in front of one of the big J5 0-6-0s built by the MGWR immediately before the Amalgamation.
[H. C. Casserley]

More revolutionary were the Drum battery electrics. The first was a conversion of Drewry car No. 386, and when this proved successful a full size articulated unit 'A' was built in 1932. [CIE]

Despite the railcar experiments, the GWR continued to produce steam engines, most of them with an eye to their use on suburban services, and in 1934/5 ten J15B 0-6-0s appeared. They were a cross between the original J15s and the I3 0-6-2Ts. Unfortunately they were, in the words of R. N. Clements, 'the most universally despised engines on the GSR . . . poor feeble things', and all were scrapped by CIE between 1959 and 1962 in advance of a number of the far older original J15s. Here the last of them, No. 719, struggles up the bank between Killiney and Dalkey in August 1956 with a train made up of three ultra-wide Park Royal suburban carriages and two old ex-GSWR non-corridors.
[David Murray]

Three more units followed, B, C and D. The two latter came out in 1939 and here one of them stands at Sallina awaiting its last journey to the scrap yard at Mullingar in July 1964. CIE removed the batteries soon after the end of the Second World War and converted the cars to trailer units.
[Kevin Murray]

Another post-Amalgamation version of a GSWR design was the D4 mixed traffic 4-4-0 of 1936. Five, with outside framed bogies and window cabs, were built for secondary services. One of them stands second in line amongst three older Inchicore-built 4-4-0s at Grand Canal Street in Dublin in 1953. [Kevin Murray]

It cannot be claimed that Inchicore designs of the period 1913–36 were especially successful and by the late 1930's the GSR was hard pushed to find adequate motive power for the heavy Dublin–Cork 'Mails'. Three engines were needed to lift the train up the three miles of 1 in 60/1 in 78 out of Glanmire Road, Cork. No. 333, a D4 of 1907, withdrawn in 1959, and No. 309, a big wheeled D10 of 1903, withdrawn in 1959 pound up the bank here in July 1951 with a combined Waterford and Tralee train. [David Murray]

The bold answer for the GSR was a big new engine, capable of handling any load unaided. In an atmosphere of considerable excitement the drawing shop at Inchicore got down to work, delighted at last to be given its head after years of penny-pinching. The result was the 800 class. No. 800 *Maeve*, in the charge of Driver Broderick and Foreman Sheehan, sets out from Cork on her inaugural run on the Up Mail on 17 July 1939. *Maeve* and her two sisters, No. 801 *Macha* and No. 802 *Tailte*, proved to be Ireland's fastest and most powerful engines and dealt with every duty with economy and ease. [*The Cork Examiner*]

The Great Southern found fuel supplies greatly restricted throughout the latter part of the Second World War. Immediately afterwards the situation grew even worse and for a short period CIE converted a number of engines to oil burning. Woolwich No. 396, so equipped and marked with large white spots on her smokebox door and tender, pulls out of Galway for Dublin in 1947. [J. M. Robbins]

CIE continued the GSR's search for an alternative to the coal-fired steam engine. One answer was Bulleid's turf burner and prior to its construction an old GSWR 2-6-0, No. 356, was experimentally fitted with a Franco-Crosti boiler and fired on turf. [H. C. Casserley]

The real answer was the diesel and, after producing five 500hp Mirlees-engined shunters in 1947, Inchicore put into service in 1951 two Sulzer-powered 950hp Bo-Bo main line diesel-electrics, Nos. 1100 and 1101. Both spent their latter years on secondary freight duties as with No. 1101, renumbered B114, at Inchicore in August 1969. Although the locomotives still exist, they have not run for some time. [Michael H. C. Baker]

B114

In 1951, the first of a fleet of diesel railcars entered service, virtually identical to those introduced by the Great Northern Railway the previous year. Built by Park Royal, with AEC engines, there were eventually 66 of these, including six built by CIE and in their early years these units worked every type of passenger service over the entire CIE system. Here a seven-car unit is on a Dublin–Cork express. In later years they were confined to the Dublin suburban lines and by early 1975 only eight remained. [CIE]

For a little while after the advent of the railcars, steam continued to make a brave show on the top-link workings left to it. Above, No. 802 *Tailte* storms past milepost 4¼ with the down Night Mail in June 1955. Below, No. 502 leaving Mallow with the up Day Mail on Easter Monday, 1956. [David Murray]

By the end of 1956, steam had vanished from all principal CIE main line duties. The first production diesel-electrics arrived from England in July 1955 and by January 1957 all 60 of these 1,200hp A Class Co-Cos were in service. They were built by Metro-Cammell and fitted with Crossley marine type engines. No. A16 heads a Cobh–Cork train in August 1969. [Michael H. C. Baker]

▶ The smaller versions of the A Class were the 550hp C Class, Bo-Bos intended primarily for branch line work. There were 33 of them, delivery beginning early in 1957. The first of these, No. C201, in original silver livery, stands in front of the soon-to-be-redundant coaling tower at Inchicore in April 1960. [Kevin Murray]

C201

Dieselisation even spread to what remained of the narrow gauge; two of the three 230hp Gardner-engined Walker B-Bs for the West Clare at Inchicore in March 1955 before entering service. [Kevin Murray]

Elsewhere steam was still alive and one could find such scenes as these in the middle and late 1950's. Above, at Inchicore in June 1954; from front to rear, a D 14 Class 4-4-0, two J 15s, a Woolwich (minus its tender), a D 2 4-4-0, 500 and 400 Class 4-6-0s. Below, Cork shed in August 1959; from left to right, a J 15, an ex-MGWR J 26 0-6-0T of 1891, a Woolwich, another J 26, a Bandon 4-6-0T and No. 100, an Inchicore-built 0-6-0T of 1891. [Michael H. C. Baker]

256
98

Bulleid, on the left, demonstrates his turf burner, the last of his many remarkable steam engines, to a visiting French engineer. The turf burner was first steamed in 1957. She performed promisingly but it was too late to save steam and CC1, as she was known, never went into revenue earning service. She was eventually dismantled, her massive chassis still surviving at Inchicore. [CIE]

Steam locomotives continued to be overhauled at Inchicore throughout the 1950's. One of the last 'Woolwichs' to remain in service, No. 385 (scrapped in 1960), makes a brave sight freshly outshopped in the lined black livery applied to a few engines in later years. [*The Cork Examiner*]

Courtmacsherry Regatta, August Bank Holiday 1955. Passengers alight at this small West Cork resort from an excursion train hauled by 0-6-0Ts Nos. 90 and 100. The former was originally part of an 0-6-4T rail motor, built for the Castleisland branch in 1875. She is now preserved at Mallow. No. 100 was built in 1891 and withdrawn in 1959. [*The Cork Examiner*]

Diesels appeared on the Courtmacsherry branch in 1958 and No. C210 is seen passing Timoleague with the August Bank Holiday special of that year. This branch closed in March 1961. [*The Cork Examiner*]

On the opposite side of the country another C Class stands at Dun Laoghaire Pier in August 1969 with a boat train for Heuston, conveying passengers from the British Rail steamer *Hibernia* which has just docked from Holyhead. [Michael H. C. Baker]

In the last years of steam, many passenger engines found themselves relegated to less exacting duties; 400 Class No. 402 pulls out of Cork with the overnight goods for Dublin in August 1959. This 4-6-0 was scrapped two years later. [Michael H. C. Baker]

Despite dieselisation, the 1950's were in many ways a period of decline and retreat. There were wholesale closures and the very existence of the railways in Ireland was threatened. The crew of the last train on the Macroom line pose around former WLWR 4-4-2T No. 269 in November 1953.
[*The Cork Examiner*]

Demolition of the roundhouse at Broadstone on July 1961. [Kevin Murray]

Two 4-4-0s awaiting breaking-up at Limerick in September 1959. No. 93 was built at Inchicore in 1885, rebuilt as a compound in 1894 and converted back to a simple in 1901. No. 344 was one of the Great Southern engines of 1936. [Michael H. C. Baker]

One of the last surviving sections of track at Broadstone, almost hidden in the long grass, August 1969. Beyond are derelict single deck buses, Leyland Tigers and Royal Tigers with CIE-built bodies dating from the late 1940's and the early 1950's. Although this is a book about railways, it would hardly be complete without a look at the extensive road fleet of CIE. [Michael H. C. Baker]

The outbreak of the Second World War prolonged the life of the Dublin trams and a number remained in service when the Dublin United Transport Company merged with the Great Southern to form CIE. Here two trams pass in the North Circular Road in the late 1930's. [J. P. Odea]

The Dublin United Transport Company introduced its first double deck buses in December 1937. Leyland Titans with Leyland bodywork were later produced to the same basic design by the DUTC; one of the 1940 batch stands alongside an early post-war OPD1 in O'Connell Street in September 1959. [Michael H. C. Baker]

An all-Leyland PD2 of 1949 leads a group of CIE vehicles in O'Connell Street.

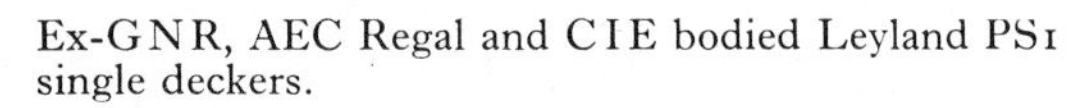

Ex-GNR, AEC Regal and CIE bodied Leyland PS1 single deckers.

A modern AEC and two modern Leyland lorries.

The latest VAN ooL bodied Leyland long distance bus and a VAN ooL/Leyland touring coach.

Inside Broadstone. A group of new buses and coaches, including a standard C I E bodied Leyland Atlantean under construction.

A CIE bodied Leyland Titan PD2 sporting a Supertrain advertisement.

A Royal Tiger touring coach of 1954; in the foreground, a Bedford schoolbus.

A view from a GNR train crossing a temporary bridge—the original one having been washed away by floods—over the River Tolka outside Amiens Street station in Dublin in 1955. The narrow bodied carriage is of interest in that it is one of a number of ex-LNWR ones bought from the LMS in the 1940's and remounted on 5ft 3in bogies. By this date the GNR was in severe financial straits and its days numbered. [Kevin Murray]

A view from the Rosslare–Cork boat train west of Dungarvan in August 1961. Even at this late date and with a diesel at the head, CIE could find nothing more up to date for four of the first five carriages than specimens dating from between 1902 and 1926. [Michael H. C. Baker]

In 1958 the GNR was divided between the Ulster Transport Authority and CIE. Compound 4-4-0 No. 85 *Merlin*, passing a CIE railcar at Mosney holiday camp, is in charge of a Belfast–Dublin express. Behind, across Dundalk Bay, the Mountains of Mourne are faintly visible. *Merlin* is now preserved and it is hoped she will be displayed at the Belfast Transport Museum. [Kevin Murray]

U Class 4-4-0 No. 197 *Lough Neagh* of 1915, with a tender from one of the 1948 engines of the same class, arriving at Amiens Street with a stopping train from Drogheda in September 1959. Apart from the CIE stencilled on the buffer beam, her livery is unaltered from GNR days but the carriages have been painted in CIE green. At the time, CIE owned another No. 197, a J15 0-6-0; the 4-4-0 was withdrawn in 1965. [Michael H. C. Baker]

Former GNR T2 4-4-2T No. 67 leaving Amiens Street with a Howth train in September 1959, No. 67 was built in 1924 and withdrawn in 1960. [Michael H. C. Baker]

No. 81, one of the UG 0-6-0 goods engines of the former GNR, leaving Amiens Street in September 1959 with a main line stopping train. No. 81 was built in 1937 and withdrawn in 1960.
[Michael H. C. Baker]

The only diesel locomotive the GNR owned was a German-built MAK 800hp 0-8-0 diesel-mechanical, delivered in 1954. Photographed at Inchicore in August 1974, this is the last former GNR locomotive on either CIE or Northern Ireland Railways books, although this unit has done little work in recent years. [Michael H. C. Baker]

A surprising development in the summer of 1974 was the overhaul and return to service of four of the later ex-GNR BUT railcars. No. 712 is seen here at Inchicore, freshly outshopped. [Michael H. C. Baker]

The interior of the former SLNCR Walker railcar, bought by CIE and renumbered 2509. It is still in existence but has been little used of late. [E. N. Calvert-Harrison]

CIE began to withdraw the GNR-built railcars in the late 1960s; a line of them stand derelict at Drogheda in August 1973. [Michael H. C. Baker]

Intermediate in power between the A and the C Class was the B of 960hp. Following on the first two of 1951 came twelve more in 1956. These, Nos. B101–112, possessed the same Sulzer power unit but the locomotives themselves were A1A-A1As built by the Birmingham Railway Carriage Wagon Company. Nowadays they are confined to freight and shunting duties between and around Cork and Dublin. No. B107 climbs towards Clasnevin Junction in August 1970 with a transfer freight from North Wall. [Michael H. C. Baker]

In 1961 a third variation of the B Class arrived. This was the General Motors 950hp Bo-Bo. No. B131 of the original, single cab batch crosses the River Barrow on the borders of Counties Laois and Kildare in the summer of 1972. [Ron Elsdon]

The most successful of all CIE's diesels and the mainstay of the fleet have been the 49 double-cab GMs. A one-off General Motors design especially for CIE, they arrived in two lots. First, in 1962, came Nos. B141–177, 950hp units, and they were followed in 1966 by Nos. B181–192, virtually identical machines but uprated to 1,100hp. At Tralee on a sunny Sunday morning in August 1974 are two of each type, the 950hp locomotives on the left, the 1,100hp ones, in the new livery introduced with the Supertrains in 1972–3, on the right. [Michael H. C. Baker]

187
CIE

CIE quickly stamped its mark on the former GNR Dublin–Belfast 'Enterprise' express. Railcars were replaced by locomotive-hauled stock and in a few years hardly any GNR-built rolling stock remained on the service. Early in their career the power units of the A Class diesel-electrics began to give trouble and from 1968 they were replaced with General Motors 1,325hp engines. Rebuilt No. A4r in charge of the southbound 'Enterprise' is approaching Dundalk in August 1971. In the background is the 1893, mountain Slieve Gullion in County Armagh, across the Northern Ireland border. [Michael H. C. Baker]

The Northern Ireland Railways shares the 'Enterprise' workings with the CIE. Its train of modified British Rail Mark 11B stock, headed by Hunslet 1,350hp Bo-Bo diesel-electric No. 103 *Merlin*, introduced in 1970, accelerates out of Amiens Street, now renamed Connolly. [Michael H. C. Baker]

Double-headed by two GMs, the northbound 'Enterprise' passes Malahide in the spring of 1970. By then the only GNR-built carriage in its formation was the buffet car, 268N, built in 1950. [Ron Elsdon]

Following the successful rebuilding of the A Class, the underpowered and unreliable C Class followed suit, being equipped with General Motors 950hp units. They retained their original numbers but the C prefix gave way to B. No. B203 stands in the former DSER section of Connolly station prior to taking a suburban working in August 1972. [Michael H. C. Baker]

Across the River Liffey from Connolly station is Pearse, formerly Westland Row station, now use almost exclusively for suburban traffic. No. A6 departs with a train for Bray in December 196 Below, passengers at Pearse. [Michael H. C. Bake

PLATFORM
2
A6

TRAINS TIMETABLE
DUBLIN SUBURBAN
TRAINS TIMETABLE
TRAINS TIMETABLE

August Bank Holiday crowds at Bray, 1971. CIE trains carry Dubliners in their thousands to this popular resort on fine summer weekends. [Michael H. C. Baker]

After decades of decline, the increasingly congested roads have brought passengers back to the suburban trains. By the late 1960' the faithful railcars were wearing out and replacement parts were virtually unobtainable. It was realised that the problem of commut traffic in Greater Dublin would have to be looked at as a whole and this might eventually mean the construction of an undergrour railway plus the electrification of the present surface lines. But as a stopgap measure most of the CIE-built railcars were convert to push–pull units powered by the re-engined C Class. One such unit passes the Grand Canal Street sidings outside Pearse static under a threatening sky in August 1973. [Michael H. C. Bake

To handle the extra summer suburban traffic, CIE kept a number of secondary stock carriages, numbered in the 4000 series, available. Here the last complete set of wooden bodied vehicles, dating from late GSWR and early GSR days, gets the right away from Pearse station on its way to Howth in August 1972. This was its last year of service.
[Michael H. C. Baker]

The biggest carriage building programme since before the Amalgamation was announced by CIE in 1970; 73 air-conditioned (AC) vehicles were ordered from British Rail Engineering at a cost approaching £3 million. Modified British Rail Mark 11Ds, they began to go into service in complete sets, known as Supertrains, in December 1972. A newly introduced rake of AC stock stands inside refurbished Heuston station in August 1973. [Michael H. C. Baker]

B150
25

Two locomotive-hauled suburban trains, with wide-bodied Park Royal-designed carriages prominent, passing outside Connolly station in August 1973. [Michael H. C. Baker]

A number of English companies had interests in Irish railways, amongst them the LNWR. Standard CIE built, Maybach engined diesel-hydraulic 400hp shunter of 1961 in the former LNWR yard at North Wall, September 1967. [Michael H. C. Baker]

The Tralee–Dublin Mail below the Stack Mountains, County Kerry, in August 1974. The leading carriage dates from the early 1950's, the next two are lightweight vehicles of 1956, then comes a Craven-designed standard of 1964—immediate predecessor of the AC stock—followed by a luggage van of the late 1950's, the State Saloon of 1902, a former British Railways Mark 1 corridor converted to a GSV steam heating brake van, and a parcels van, formerly a GSR corridor built in the late 1930's. [Michael H. C. Baker]

A former GSWR combined goods and cattle wagon and a former GSWR goods van at Achill in 1934. Both are in pre-1925 livery.
[H. C. Casserley]

A former GSWR four plank coal wagon at Limerick, July 1934. [H. C. Casserley]

Tralee & Dingle wagons and carriages at Dingle, July 1934.
[H. C. Casserley]

Cattle traffic was one of the chief revenue earners for the railways in Ireland for over a century but it has declined steadily since the Amalgamation and may well shortly disappear altogether. The stationmaster at Tralee inspects a derailed cattle truck during an August downpour.
[Michael H. C. Baker]

A former GSWR horsebox and standard GSWR brake van at Heuston, August 1973.
[Michael H. C. Baker]

North Wall, Dublin. Prominent amongst the various types of wagons in this view taken in August 1973 are containers mounted on four wheel flats which normally run in liner trains. Already these are being replaced by bogie vehicles and CIE plans to make block trains universal, thus abolishing the non-braked four wheeler—except for the seasonal beet traffic—and removing the need for shunting. [Michael H. C. Baker]

A train load of Guinness, carried in specially designed wagons, being shunted at the Guinness sidings at Heuston.
[Michael H. C. Baker]

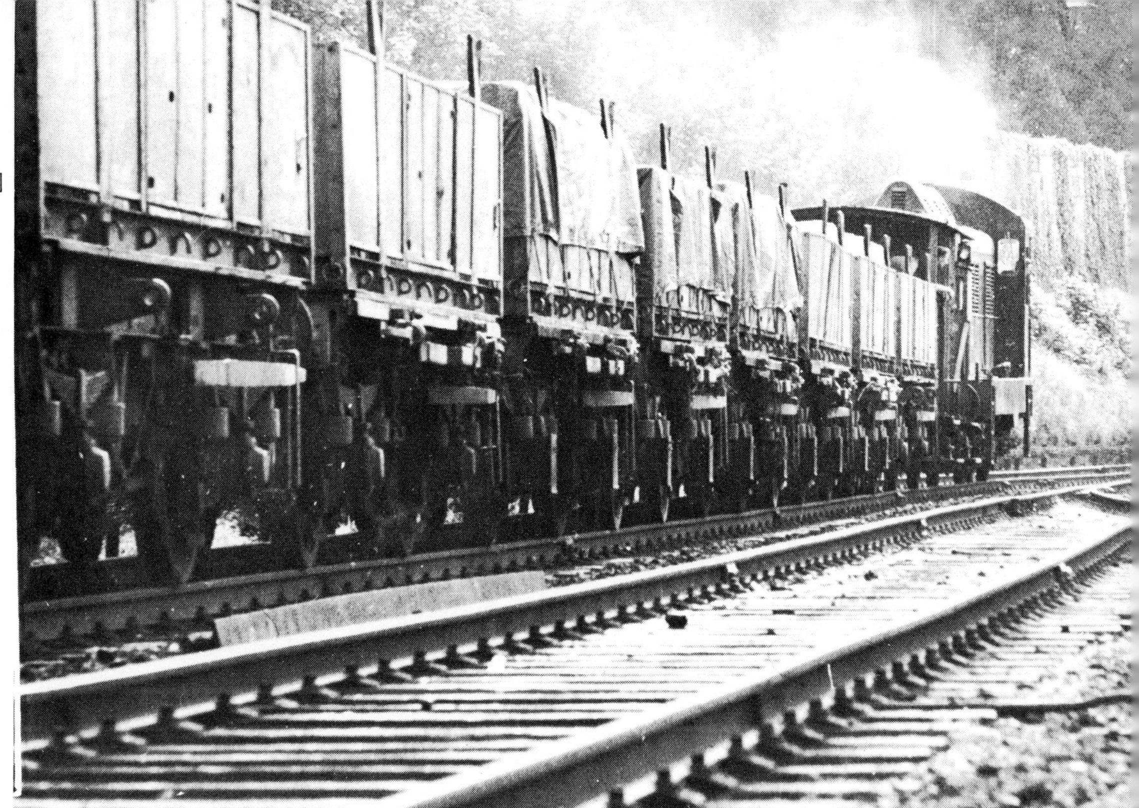

Photographed at Inchicore in August 1974, before entering service, is a wagon of a type introduced in that year for carrying palletised bagged fertiliser. Its bogies are of French design.
[Michael H. C. Baker]

The thrice-weekly North Kerry goods, hauled by a GM Class 950hp Bo-Bo, on the climb out of Tralee in August 1974. Behind are the mountains of the Dingle Peninsula.
[Michael H. C. Baker]

It will be some time before the loose-coupled, traditional pick-up goods train disappears in Ireland. One waits for the road at Islandbridge, outside Heuston, hauled by No. B114 in August 1970. The tall building in the background is Liberty Hall, headquarters of the Trade Union Movement.
[Michael H. C. Baker]

Inchicore, August 1974. The remains of No. 008, brought back and dumped alongside one of the original CIE Mirrlees-engined shunters of 1947. No. 008 was blown up by terrorists on 23 October 1973 near the Border whilst working an overnight Dundalk-Belfast liner train.
[Michael H. C. Baker]

Connolly, August 1971; refugees from the bombing in Belfast raise a smile for the camera as their special train pauses for refreshments on its way south.
[Michael H. C. Baker]

Preservation; far and away the oldest surviving Irish locomotive in Ireland is Bury 2-2-2 No. 36 built for the GSWR in 1848 and now preserved at Kent station, Cork. [Michael H. C. Baker]

The Railway Preservation Society of Ireland has achieved wonders despite immense difficulties and has a fine and growing collection of locomotives, carriages and wagons kept at its headquarters at Whitehead in Northern Ireland. From time to time one of its tours visits the Republic and here preserved J15 0-6-0 No. 186 heads south through the Dublin suburbs. [Ron Elsdon]

The RPSI also own a former NCC 2-6-4T No. 4—the Irish version of the standard LMS 2-6-4T —seen here passing Glasnevin on the Dublin loop line. [Ron Elsdon]

The Glasnevin and Drumcondra Loop line joins the former GSWR main line at Islandbridge, immediately north of Heuston station. No. A18R swings through the junction with an up Galway train and crosses the Liffey, her headlights on in preparation for the Phoenix Park tunnel which she is about to enter. [Ron Elsdon]

Renumbered and repainted AR Class locomotives Nos. 027 and 041 wait at Islandbridge on Christmas Eve 1973 preparatory to backing down to Heuston and taking out holiday trains to the West. This was one of the busiest Christmases ever for CIE with the fuel crisis bringing many extra passengers. [Michael H. C. Baker]

A line of open and covered four-wheel cattle wagons—a sight familiar since the beginnings of Irish railways but one which will soon belong to the past—alongside a Supertrain, CIE's standard passenger carriages for the future; Tralee, August 1974. [Michael H. C. Baker]